# Unleashing Your Entrepreneurship Spirit

# Unleashing Your Entrepreneurship Spirit

## TAKE THE PLUNGE

LYNETTE MARSHALL-HARPER

*Unleashing Your Entrepreneurial Spirit*

Copyright © 2023 by Lynette Marshall-Harper

Book Production:
Marvin D. Cloud, mybestseller Publishing Company
marvindcloud@gmail.com

# Dedication

*To my beloved husband, Earl Harper, who has been my unwavering support and the rock on which I build my dreams. Your love and encouragement has been my constant inspiration.*

*To my daughters, soon-to-be Dr. Donica Harper and Alexandra Harper, who embody the values of hard work and determination. Your accomplishments fill me with pride, and I'm excited to witness the incredible journeys that lie ahead for both of you.*

*To my loving grandson, Dakari Henry, whose infectious joy and curiosity reminds me of the beauty in life's simplest moments. May you always chase your dreams with the same enthusiasm.*

*This book is dedicated to my family, whose love and belief in me have made this journey possible.*

# Acknowledgments

Bringing *Unleashing Your Entrepreneurial Spirit* to life has been a remarkable journey. Without the help of many incredible individuals, it wouldn't have been possible.

First and foremost, I extend my deepest gratitude to my mentors, Dr. Lynn Richardson and Toni Harris Taylor, whose wisdom and guidance have guided my path to growth and success. Your mentorship has not only expanded my horizons but also enriched my life in ways I could never have imagined.

To my friends and colleagues who have shared their wisdom, experiences, and valuable insight, I thank you for your support and encouragement.

I extend my appreciation to my book producer and editor, Marvin D. Cloud. Your professionalism and dedication transformed my manuscript into a tangible reality. Your commitment to the craft of publishing is evident on every page.

Lastly, to the readers of this book, thank you for embarking on this journey with me. I hope that the words within these pages ignite the entrepreneurial spirit within you and empower you to pursue your dreams fearlessly.

—*Lynette Marshall-Harper*

# Contents

# Introduction

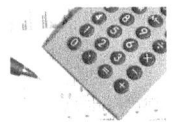

Entrepreneurship stands as a beacon of innovation, a symbol of resilience, and a testament to the indomitable spirit of those who dare to dream. It's a journey where creativity meets determination, uncertainty meets opportunity, and passion meets purpose. Welcome to *Unleashing Your Entrepreneurship Spirit*, an expedition into the hearts and soul of entrepreneurship.

This book is a guide for those who seek to embark on the exhilarating path of entrepreneurship and for those who are already on this remarkable voyage. Whether you're a wide-eyed dreamer with a groundbreaking idea, a seasoned businessperson looking to reinvent yourself, or somewhere in between, the pages that follow will offer insights, wisdom, and inspiration to fuel your entrepreneurial spirit.

Why entrepreneurship? Because it's more than just starting a business; it's a way of thinking, seeing the world, and taking action. It's about bringing your vision to life, creating value where there was none, and leaving an indelible mark on the world. Entrepreneurship is about embracing challenges and uncertainties, knowing that the seeds of your success lie within them.

This book will cover the mindset that supports innovation, the methods that lead to growth, and the resilience that helps you weather adversity. We'll celebrate the spirit of entrepreneurship, the audacious spirit that turns dreams into reality and defies the odds. When nurtured, it can unleash boundless potential.

Whether you're in pursuit of a lifelong dream or curious about what it takes to be an entrepreneur, the journey ahead will be challenging. However, it will also be immensely rewarding. It's a journey that demands courage, creativity, and an unwavering belief in your ability to make a difference. Are you ready to unleash your entrepreneurship spirit? If so, let's embark on this transformational voyage together.

# Chapter 1: Mindset Shift

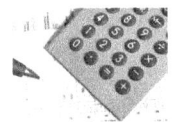

Writing a book was never on my radar. It wasn't a dream or aspiration I had ever entertained. Yet here I am, working on my third book. How did I end up on this unexpected path? Let me share my story.

The year 2020 brought about tremendous challenges and devastation with the global pandemic. The pandemic did not cause financial hardships for my family, unlike many others. It was during this time of reflection that I realized the power of my side hustles and multiple income streams in building financial wealth. I discovered I had unknowingly been on the right track all along, but on the wrong train. This realization ignited a thirst for knowledge about financial freedom. It also gave me the desire to leave a lasting legacy for my family through entrepreneurship.

But writing a book? That thought had never crossed my mind until my mentor, Toni Harris Taylor, suggested it. I must admit, I thought she was a bit crazy. What wisdom or insight could I possibly offer to help others? Doubt crept in, and I confided in my friend, Dianne, expressing my reservations.

"I'm not an author," I told her. "I have no idea where to begin when it comes to writing a book." Dianne, however, saw something in me I couldn't see in myself.

She reminded me of my unique ability to help people unravel their thoughts and ideas, particularly when starting a business. Her suggestion intrigued me. It seemed far-fetched at first, but the more I thought about it, the more it made sense. I realized I needed to shift my mindset about who I believed myself to be and recognize the value I could bring to others through my experiences and insights.

With trepidation and a newfound sense of purpose, I embarked on this unexpected journey of writing a book. I had to confront my self-doubt, challenge my preconceived notions, and embrace the idea that I could make a difference in the lives of others. Through this process, I discovered that sometimes our true purpose lies just beyond our comfort zones, waiting to be unlocked. But to unlock that power, I had to change my mindset, harness my potential, and empower myself to discover my entrepreneurial spirit.

Embarking on the entrepreneurial path requires more than a business plan or a brilliant idea. One of the most significant factors that determines success is your mindset. Mindset plays a crucial role in shaping your success as an entrepreneur. It's important to understand how changing your mindset can transform you before starting a business.

Let's look at some ways to help lay a solid foundation for starting a business and thriving as an entrepreneur. Prepare to unlock the doors to your potential and embrace the unexpected to leave a lasting impact on others. The time for change and impact is now.

1. **Overcoming barriers.** Identify and question what is holding you back from starting a business. Reflect on any fears, doubts, or limiting beliefs that might prevent you from taking a leap into entrepreneurship. Look for any challenges or assumptions that may hinder your progress.

2. **Self-Imposed limitations.** Understand that limitations are often self-imposed, but you can overcome them. Recognize that many limitations are not inherent, but self-imposed beliefs about what you can or cannot achieve. Overcome limitations by seeking inspiration from successful entrepreneurs and building a supportive network.

3. **Cultivating optimism.** Foster optimism and see opportunities where others see obstacles. Cultivate an optimistic mindset to see possibilities and potential where others may only see challenges. Develop a mindset that sees obstacles as opportunities for growth and approach problems focusing on finding solutions.

4. **Positive attitude**. Create a can-do attitude and maintain resilience when facing challenges. That type of attitude drives you to take action, persist in adversity, and create solutions for problems. Maintain resilience. View setbacks as temporary learning experiences that provide valuable lessons for future success.

5. **Calculated risk.** Recognize that calculated risk is essential for entrepreneurial success. Understand that entrepreneurship inherently involves taking risks. Successful entrepreneurs approach risk-taking in a calculated manner. To manage risk, research, gather information, and make informed decisions. Embrace a mindset that understanding calculated risk is necessary to achieve significant rewards.

6. **Setbacks.** Understand that setbacks are a natural part of the entrepreneurial journey. Accept that setbacks and challenges are part of the entrepreneurial journey. Don't get discouraged by setbacks. Use them to learn, grow and become more resilient. Maintain a long-term perspective and focus on the lessons learned from setbacks to make improvements and move forward.

7. **Knowledge and skill.** Understand that knowledge and skill are critical assets to entrepreneurship. Commit to acquiring industry-specific knowledge, staying updated on market trends, and enhancing relevant necessary skills for your business. This ongoing investment in your own development will contribute to your success as an entrepreneur.

8. **Personal and professional growth.** Commit to personal and professional development. Make a deliberate commitment to your personal and professional growth. Seek opportunities for learning, whether through courses, workshops, networking events, or mentorship. Continuously challenge yourself. Set goals, and actively work

towards improving your entrepreneurial skills, mindset, and overall well-being.

Starting a business demands a fundamental shift in mindset. Be open to new possibilities, have an entrepreneurial mindset, and focus on growth. This will help you overcome challenges, seize opportunities, and succeed in business. Remember, your mindset is the compass that guides your entrepreneurial journey, so nurture it with care and determination.

# Chapter 2: The Power of Multiple Streams of Income

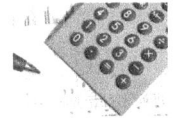

In the previous chapter, I shared my journey of self-discovery and the realization that I had been on the right track all along, just on the wrong train. The journey led me to uncover the concept of "Multiple Streams of Income." This is a powerful principle that would transform my financial outlook and entrepreneurial pursuits. Although I always had an inclination toward side hustles, I was unaware of the true potential of multiple income streams.

As a child, I learned about entrepreneurship, but I didn't comprehend the significance of diversifying income sources. Let me explain the concept of multiple streams of income for those who may be in a similar position.

Simply put, multiple streams of income means earning money from several sources. Multiple streams of income are not only about financial security; it creates an environment where you can focus on what truly matters to you. It involves tapping into activities that bring you joy and fulfillment, allowing you to impact others positively.

Whether it's offering services or selling products, your passion can become a means of generating income.

I came to realize that the average millionaire has at least seven sources of income. Following this blueprint can lead to financial success. So, how can you generate passive income?

My mentor, Lynn Richardson, always says, "Learn the rules of the game and play by the rules of the game." This led me to invest in myself and seek knowledge from those willing to share their expertise.

Here's the truth. Seeking knowledge may come at a cost, but the value of investing in yourself far outweighs the price of achieving financial freedom. In life, nothing is entirely free; everything comes at a cost. Embracing the mindset of growth and investing in your own development can pave the way to prosperity and create a legacy for the future.

Achieving financial freedom is a common aspiration for many entrepreneurs. Relying solely on a single income stream can limit your potential and leave you vulnerable to economic fluctuations. This section highlights the drawbacks of relying on a single income source and the advantages of having multiple revenue streams.

1. **Increase financial security.** By diversifying your income, you reduce the risk of solely depending on one income stream. If one source of income is affected, you have other sources to rely on. That diminishes the impact of financial setbacks and ensures a more stable financial situation.

2. **Flexibility and adaptability.** Multiple income streams allow you to be more flexible and adaptable to changing circumstances. Should one income stream become less profitable, or no longer align with your goals, you can shift your focus to other sources of income. You can do this without significant disruption to your overall financial well-being.

3. **Income growth potential.** Multiple income streams provide the opportunity for increased earning potential. Work to grow and expand income sources through various methods. This can accelerate your overall financial growth and create more wealth accumulation opportunities.

4. **Risk reduction.** Different income streams often have different risk profiles. By diversifying, you can balance higher-risk ventures with more static and predictable

income sources. Helping to mitigate the impact of potential losses in one area with gains from others, reducing risk exposure.

5. **Peace of mind.** Knowing your financial well-being is not solely dependent on a single income source can give you peace of mind. It can also alleviate stress, increase confidence, and provide a sense of security. This will allow you to focus on personal and professional goals without the constant worry about financial stability.

6. **Entrepreneurial opportunities.** Starting your own business or engaging in side projects can provide opportunities for additional income. Having an entrepreneurial mindset can promote creativity, innovation, and self-reliance. It permits you to pursue your interests, use your abilities, and potentially earn more money by expanding your business.

Relying on a single income stream limits your financial potential, and it exposes you to unnecessary risks. To achieve financial freedom, you need to diversify your income streams and explore different sources of revenue. You can build a foundation for financial stability and abundance by realizing the diversification.

The idea of multiple income streams, and exploring various sources of revenue is important. A diversified income portfolio can give you more earning potential and security. Managing multiple income streams demands planning, time management, resilience, and dedication. It may involve juggling different responsibilities and balancing various income sources.

# Chapter 3: Liberating Yourself from the 9-to-5 Job Curse

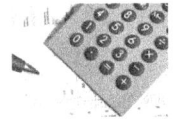

Leaving a lasting legacy for our family involves more than just leaving behind money; it encompasses a blueprint for achieving financial freedom and security. In my journey, I came to understand the true concept of financial freedom in my late forties. Prior to that, life had kept me busy raising a family, pursuing education, working my 9-to-5 job, and hustling on the side. It wasn't until I faced significant financial challenges that I realized the importance of securing my family's future.

Living paycheck to paycheck, buried under bills, and facing foreclosure, I knew I had to take charge and get my financial life in order. With my financial strategy and analysis skills, I improved my family's financial situation through hard work. Once we achieved stability, I shared this newfound knowledge with my daughter, encouraging her to start her own business.

Amidst the pandemic, my daughter took a leap of faith and left her 9-to-5 job to start a practice in the mental health industry. While her business required minimal startup funds, she was well prepared. She saved enough money to cover her expenses for four months. Then she crafted a business plan, devised marketing strategies, and collaborated with others in the same field.

For my daughter, leaving her 9-to-5 job and embracing entrepreneurship turned out to be the best decision she ever made. The rewards go beyond financial gains. My daughter enjoys helping people with mental health issues and it allows her to be creative and persistent.

She learned that failure is a step toward success, and adaptability is a form of resiliency. Her journey exemplifies the transformative power of entrepreneurship. It includes the freedom of charting your journey, the power in alignment, and the potential it holds to create a legacy of meaningful impact.

In this pursuit of financial freedom and leaving a legacy, we learn that it's not just about the money we accumulate. But it is also the knowledge and empowerment we pass down to future generations. By fostering an entrepreneurial mindset and taking calculated risks, we can pave the way for a more secure and prosperous future. This isn't just for ourselves but for our loved ones as well.

They taught me to go to school, get an education, and get a job. This leads to grinding for someone else for 10, 20, sometimes 30 years and no generational wealth at the end of the tunnel. But I would not feed my daughters this pipe dream. Instead, I have given them the blueprint to be free from the 9-to-5 job curse so they can seek greater flexibility, freedom, and fulfillment. While leaving the security of a steady job to work for yourself is a bold and transformative decision. There are steps you can take to work towards this goal. Here are some strategies to consider:

1. **Identify your passion and purpose.** What are your interests, values, and skills? What truly motivates you? Understanding your passion and purpose will guide you toward entrepreneurship that aligns with your aspirations.

2. **Set clear goals.** Define your goals and create a roadmap to reach your objectives. Set short-term and long-term goals that are specific, measurable, attainable, and relevant. Breaking them down into actionable steps can make them more manageable.

3. **Develop new skills.** Find out what skills and knowledge you need for your desired

path. Take courses, attend workshops, seek mentorship, or explore online resources to learn and enhance your expertise. Relevant skills will boost your confidence and increase your chances of success.

4. **Build a financial cushion.** Before leaving your 9-to-5 job, it's essential to establish a financial safety net. Save a sufficient amount of money to cover your living expenses for at least six months to a year. Consider potential business startup costs or transitional periods without a regular income.

5. **Create a transition plan.** Rather than abruptly quitting your job, consider transitioning gradually. This approach allows you to test the waters, gain experience, and build a network before fully leaping to entrepreneurship.

6. **Network and collaborate.** Connect with like-minded individuals in your desired industry. Attend industry events, join online forums, and engage in networking activities to build relationships and learn from others who have successfully made the transition. Collaborations and partnerships can offer valuable support and opportunities.

7. **Remote work and subcontracting**.
   Remote work and sub-contracting have become more accessible than ever. Explore opportunities to work remotely as a subcontractor or find remote positions within your field. This flexibility can provide more control over your schedule and location.

8. **Prioritize self-care and work-life balance.**
   Prioritize self-care and maintain a healthy work-life balance as you move away from traditional work structures. Rest, do enjoyable activities, connect with others, and practice mindfulness for your well-being.

Releasing yourself from the 9-to-5 job curse requires careful planning, dedication, and perseverance. Breaking free from the job mentality requires self-belief, resilience, and a willingness to step outside your comfort zone. This will help you create a life and career that truly align with your passions and aspirations. It may not happen overnight, but by taking consistent steps toward your goals, you can gradually create a more fulfilling and flexible work life. After all, the goal is to get in alignment with what you want for yourself and your family.

# Chapter 4: Skill Set, Passion, and Purpose

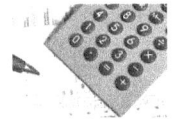

Skill set, passion, and purpose are powerful individual characteristics. However, they can be life-changing when harnessed collectively. As a teenager, I always found myself drawn to helping my friends with their problems, and I took immense pleasure in solving puzzles and figuring things out. This inclination to assist others in need, is a trait undoubtedly inherited from my grandmother. All knew and loved her as the neighborhood's Big Mama. She guided my journey into adulthood.

As I grew, my passion for helping others and my analytical mind naturally steered me toward a career in accounting. It felt like a perfect alignment of my skills and my desire to affect people's lives positively.

Compared to finding your true purpose, knowing your skills and passions is simple. Many individuals leave this world without fully grasping their purpose. Finding your purpose involves contributing to the greater good in ways that align with your skills, strengths, passions, and values.

'It's important to identify the cause and issues that matter to you, the injustices you wish to fix, and the satisfaction you feel when helping others. This is part of envisioning the life you wish to lead.

I've witnessed the journey of purpose in my youngest daughter, who was intense and struggled with self-esteem and anxiety as a child. Despite her challenges, she never allowed them to hinder her progress.

During the pandemic, she completed her Master's degree, and recently made the bold move to quit her job and start her own business as a Virtual Assistant. This gave her a more flexible schedule to coach cheerleaders. Her decision was driven by her passion for helping young girls build their self-esteem through cheerleading.

Beyond her professional pursuits, this drastic move granted her the opportunity to be fully present in her four-year-old son's life. It allowed her to partake in the myriad of events and experiences that her previous full-time job could not provide.

We all have a purpose in life, but it's up to each of us to discover it. Your purpose is unique to you, and it requires deliberate effort to seek and embrace. Remember, everyone has a purpose, and sometimes, our paths may intersect with others who share similar journeys. Embrace the unknown with courage, for it is often in those uncharted territories that we find the greatest joy and fulfillment.

In the pursuit of purpose, we become architects of our own destiny. We weave together our skill set, passion, and values to create a meaningful life that leaves a lasting impact on others and the world. Embrace the journey, for within it lies the key to unlocking the true potential of your purpose on this earth.

Thus, skill set, passion, and purpose are three distinct but interconnected elements. They are crucial in shaping your career and overall fulfillment. It is the backbone of your entrepreneurial journey and success and where you discover most of your joy in owning your own business. Let us explore each one:

1.  **Skill set.** Refers to the specific abilities, knowledge, and expertise developed through education, training, and experience. Understanding your skill set is vital, as it forms the foundation of your professional capabilities. It can guide you in identifying entrepreneurial opportunities where you can enhance your skills.

2.  **Passion.** Refers to a robust and intense enthusiasm or interest in a particular activity, topic, or field. It's something

that genuinely excites and motivates you. Discovering your passion is crucial because it can drive your career decisions and help you find work that brings you joy and fulfillment. When you are passionate about what you do, staying motivated, dedicated, and continually growing in your chosen field becomes easier.

3. **Purpose.** Relates to a more profound sense of meaning and fulfillment in your work and life. It is essential to understand the impact you want to make and align your action with your values and beliefs. Finding your purpose allows you to connect with a higher sense of purpose beyond financial rewards. It involves contributing to something larger than yourself and positively impacting others or society as a whole.

The combination of skill set, passion, and purpose is where individuals often find the most fulfillment and success as an entrepreneur. Exciting work that uses your skills and passion can bring happiness, creativity, and drive. This allows you to improve and master your craft. Utilizing your passion and purpose can give you a deeper sense.

When skill set, passion, and purpose intersect, you can build a business that leverages your expertise, aligns with your values, and brings you fulfillment. Always develop your skills, pursue your passion, and stay connected to your purpose in your entrepreneurial journey. Regularly check and improve your skills, stay enthusiastic, and remember your goals and values. Integrating skill sets, passion, and purpose is key to a thriving entrepreneurial venture.

# Chapter 5: Know Your Market and Customers

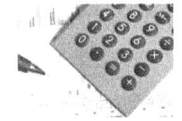

Starting your own business can be overwhelming. This is especially challenging for understanding what people want and who will buy your products and services. In the beginning, it may seem like a labyrinth of uncertainty, especially if you are new to the world of entrepreneurship. However, I assure you that this process is essential and transformative as you progress on your path.

Let me share my experience when I first started my Financial and Life Coaching business. I was clueless about understanding my targeted clients and dominating the market. But as I immersed myself in the process of discovering my customers and comprehending the market dynamics, connecting the dots, and aligning everything—my vision became easier.

Your market and customers hold the key to maximizing your revenue potential. Launching a business involves numerous aspects that contribute to its success. Therefore, it is vital to understand and embrace each step of the process. That not only makes you a better individual and professional but it also refines your proficiency.

Begin by delving into the needs of your potential customers and how your product or service can benefit them. What sets your offering apart from others in the market? These are crucial questions you must address and explore deeply to attract the individuals you intend to serve.

Knowing your ideal market and customers is key to building a successful business. Allow it to shape your entrepreneurial paradigm. It may be challenging at first. The rewards of honing your expertise and connecting with your target audience will propel your business toward success.

Knowing your market and customers is crucial to building a successful entrepreneurial business. Understanding who your target audience is, their needs, preferences, and behaviors is vital. This helps you meet their expectations by customizing your offerings and strategies. Trust the process, and let it guide you toward revenue maximization and fulfillment on your entrepreneurial path. Here are some key steps to help you know your market and customers.

1. **Market research.** Conduct market research to gain insight into the overall market

landscape, industry trends, and potential opportunities. Identify the size of your target market, its growth potential, and the competitive landscape. This research helps you understand the market dynamics and position your business effectively.

2. **Define your target audience.** Clearly define your target audience or customer segments. Consider factors such as demographics (age, gender, location, income), psychographics (values, interests, lifestyle), and behavior patterns (buying habits, preferences). Create buyer personas representing your ideal customers, including their motivations, pain points, and aspirations.

3. **Customer feedback and engagement.** Actively seek feedback from your customers and engage with them to learn about their experiences, preferences, and needs. Utilize surveys, interviews, focus groups, and social media interactions to gather insights. This feedback helps refine your products, services, and overall customer experience.

4. **Competitive analysis.** Analyze your competitors to understand their offerings,

pricing strategies, marketing approaches, strengths and weaknesses. Identify gaps in the market that you can capitalize on and determine how you can differentiate your business to stand out from the competition.

5. **Stay updated on industry trends.** Keep up with industry trends, new technologies, and changes in consumer behavior that could affect your target market. Regularly research industry publications, attend conferences or webinars, and follow thought leaders in your field. This knowledge helps you anticipate shifts in customer demands and adapt your business strategy accordingly.

6. **Customer relationship management.** Continuously nurture customer relationships by maintaining regular communication and providing excellent customer service. Listen to their feedback, address their concerns, and identify opportunities to upsell or cross-sell. A satisfied customer is more likely to become a loyal brand advocate and refer others to your business.

Investing time and effort in understanding your market and customers can help you meet their needs. This customer-centric approach enhances your chances of building a loyal customer base, achieving sustainable growth, and staying ahead of the competition. Regularly revisit and update your knowledge of the market and customers, as their needs and preferences may evolve over time.

# Chapter 6: Competitive Pricing

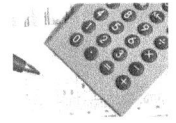

As an aspiring entrepreneur, one of the critical factors that will determine the success of your business is pricing strategy. Competitive pricing is a crucial aspect of entrepreneurship. It is an essential aspect of gaining a foothold in the market and attracting customers. Setting the right prices for your products or services can help you stand out from the competition, win over customers, and achieve sustainable growth while ensuring profitability.

One of the most crucial decisions I faced when I ventured into the world of entrepreneurship, was determining the right pricing strategy for my services. It was a difficult task, and I knew it could significantly impact the success of my business.

To begin, I conducted thorough market research by exploring the rates of other professionals in my area. Then I browsed their websites, and carefully assessed their services. I considered their education and expertise levels. Simultaneously, I analyzed the saturation of the service I intended to provide in my local area and nearby regions to gauge the level of competition. Armed with this valuable information, I strategically positioned my pricing to be competitive. It reflected the value I offered as a skilled professional. Finding that sweet spot where I could attract customers without undervaluing my expertise was essential.

I learned that it's vital to balance being competitive in the market and recognizing the worth of my skills and the value I bring to my clients. Setting the right pricing helped me establish myself among competitors and reinforced my confidence in the value of my services.

Careful competition analysis and pricing strategies can pave the way for long-term success. When this takes place, you attract customers and build a brand reputation. However, always keep a close eye on your costs and monitor customer feedback to fine-tune your pricing strategy as your business develops. Here are some considerations for implementing competitive pricing.

1. **Market research**. Conduct thorough market research to understand the pricing in your industry. Identify competitors offering similar products or services and analyze

their pricing strategies. Look at their pricing model, price ranges, and any unique value propositions they offer. This research will give info on what customers expect and how the market affects pricing decisions.

2. **Value proposition.** Determine your unique value proposition and how it differentiates you from your competitors. Assess the value you provide customers with through factors such as product quality, features, customer service, or convenience. Price your offerings to reflect this value and justify the premium you may charge compared to competitors.

3. **Cost analysis.** Understanding the costs associated with producing and delivering your products or services is vital. Consider direct costs (e.g., materials, production, labor) and indirect costs (e.g., overhead, marketing, administrative expenses). Calculate your profit margins and ensure that your pricing covers these costs while allowing for a reasonable profit.

4. **Pricing strategies.** Choose an appropriate pricing strategy that aligns with your business goals and target market. Common strategies include:

*Cost-based pricing:* Set prices based on your costs and desired profit margin. Add a markup percentage to cover expenses and ensure profitability.

*Value-based pricing:* Price based on the perceived value of your offerings to customers. Focus on your products' or services' benefits and outcomes, and set prices accordingly.

*Competitive-based pricing:* Set prices relative to your competitors. Consider whether you want to price higher, lower, or at a similar level. Be cautious with this strategy, as it may lead to price wars and erode profitability if not managed effectively.

5. **Customer perception.** Understand your target customers'' price sensitivity and willingness to pay. Consider factors such as their purchasing power, buying behaviors, and perceptions of value. Position your prices to resonate with your target market and communicate the quality, benefits, or savings they can expect from choosing your services or products. Make sure your prices reflect the needs and wants of your target market and highlight the advantages of choosing your offerings.

6. **Customer lifetime value.** Consider the long-term value of your customers beyond individual transactions. When determining your pricing strategy, factor in customer loyalty, repeat purchases, and potential referrals. Building a loyal customer base can justify offering competitive prices and lead to greater profitability over time.

7. **Flexibility and adjustments.** Monitor market trends, customer feedback, and competitor actions to stay agile with your pricing. Be open to adjusting your prices as necessary to remain competitive or respond to changes in costs or market demand. Offer discounts, promotions, or pricing incentives strategically to attract customers without compromising long-term profitability.

Competitive pricing is not solely about being the cheapest in the market. It is about finding the right balance between customer value, profitability, and market positioning. Reassess and refine your pricing strategy based on customer input and market trends. Ensure you stay competitive and maximize your business's financial performance.

# Chapter 7: One-Page Business Plan

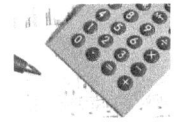

As an aspiring entrepreneur, crafting a one-page business plan only sparked in my mind when I realized its immense value in securing funding. One of my mentors also expressed the importance of a well-structured business plan. It became evident that this concise yet powerful document could be the key to attracting investors and partners who share my passion for the venture. With newfound determination, I began crafting a compelling one-page business plan that would succinctly showcase the essence of my vision, the market opportunity, and the solid strategies I intended to employ.

Throughout the process, I discovered that condensing my business ideas into one page was both a challenge and a blessing. The experience forced me to prioritize the most critical aspects of my business into clear and interesting statements. The discipline of focusing on the essentials not only refined my vision but also honed my ability to succinctly communicate it That skill would prove invaluable in the competitive business landscape.

As I dove deeper into my one-page business plan, I saw the bigger picture of my entrepreneurial journey. This document served as a roadmap. It guided me through the initial stages of launching the business and laying a solid foundation for future growth. It instilled a sense of confidence in my potential as an entrepreneur and reinforced my determination to turn my dream into reality. Armed with this concise plan, I felt ready to face the challenges ahead and secure the funding needed to unlock the full potential of my business.

You can concisely outline your business strategies and concepts with a one-page business plan. Here's a step-by-step guide to how to write a one-page business plan.

1. **Executive Summary.** Start your one-page business plan with a brief executive summary. Summarize the key points of your business, including the problem you are solving, your target market, your unique value proposition, and your competitive advantage. Keep it concise and interesting to grab the reader's attention.

2. **Business Description.** Provide a succinct description of your business. Explain what you offer, your target customer, and how your products or services meet their needs.

Highlight any unique features or benefits that set you apart from your competitors.

3. **Market Analysis.** Give a brief overview of your target market and industry. Describe the size, growth potential, and key trends in your market. Identify your target customers, their characteristics, and their buying behaviors. Highlight any market gaps or opportunities you plan to leverage.

4. **Competitive Analysis.** Briefly discuss your competition. Identify key competitors and their strengths and weaknesses. Explain how your business differentiates itself and offers a unique value proposition to attract customers.

5. **Marketing and Sales Strategy.** Outline your marketing and sales approach. Explain how you will reach and attract customers through online marketing, social media, partnerships, or other channels. Describe your pricing strategy, distribution methods, and sales tactics.

6. **Operations and Management.** Provide an overview of your business operations, including your physical location, production processes, or technology

platforms. Highlight the key members of your management team and their expertise. If relevant, mention any strategic partnership or major suppliers.

7. **Financial Projection.** Include a summary of your financial projections. Mention key financial metrics, such as revenue projections, expected expense, and profitability targets. Keep this section brief, focusing on the most critical aspects of your financial outlook.

8. **Action Plan.** Lay out the key milestones and action steps needed to launch and grow your business. Include a timeline with specific targets and deadlines. This shows your commitment to executing a coherent plan.

9. **Risks and Mitigation.** Acknowledge potential risks or challenges that your business may face, such as regulatory changes, market volatility, or competitive threats. Briefly explain how you plan to mitigate these risks or overcome challenges.

10. **Conclusion.** End your one-page business plan with a concise conclusion that reinforces the strengths of your business

concepts highlights your commitment to success and leaves a positive impression.

The one-page business plan aims to provide a high-level overview of your business and its key components. Keep your language clear and concise, focusing on the most critical information. Use bullet points, subheadings, and visual elements to make your plan easy to read and understand. Regularly review and revise your plan as your business grows and new opportunities arise.

# Chapter 8: Financial Strategy and Saving Plan

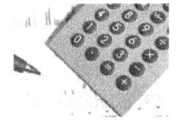

Before leaving your job to start your own business, it's a good idea to plan your finances and savings. It helps to ensure you have a solid financial foundation and will mitigate some risks associated with starting a business.

I recall when my daughter left her job to enter the world of entrepreneurship. She established a well-thought-out financial strategy and saving plan. She designed it to safeguard her financial stability during the initial state of building her business.

Her robust savings plan provided her with a safety net. It gave her peace of mind to focus on growing her business without the constant worry of immediate financial pressures. It also gave her confidence and clarity, knowing she had a backup plan and a financial cushion to rely on if unforeseen challenges arose.

A financial plan can help you show investors or lenders how your business is doing financially. This will further increase your chances of securing external funding to fuel business growth.

Having a strong savings plan reduced her financial risk. That reduced personal stress during the entrepreneurial journey. Here are some steps to consider:

1. **Assess your current financial situation.** Evaluate your current income, expenses, savings, and debts. Figure out how much money you'll need to cover your expenses during and after the transition.

2. **Set a financial goal.** Determine the amount of savings you want to accumulate before leaving your employment. This goal should include funds to cover both personal expenses and initial business expenses. It's recommended to have at least six to twelve months of living expenses saved up as a safety net.

3. **Create a budget.** Develop a budget to track your income and expenses. Identify areas where you can cut back or reduce expenses to increase your savings rate. Be mindful of your spending and prioritize savings as much as possible while still employed.

4. **Build an emergency fund.** Establish an emergency fund to handle unexpected expenses or income fluctuations. This fund

should ideally cover three to six months of living expenses. Start setting aside a portion of your income specifically for this fund.

5. **Minimize personal debt.** Consider paying off debts like credit cards and loans before becoming an entrepreneur. Reducing your personal debt burden will give you more financial flexibility and ease financial stress as you embark on your new venture.

6. **Explore health insurance options.** Research health insurance options available to you once you leave your employment. You can either check the costs and coverage of private plans or see if you qualify for government programs or professional associations. They often offer entrepreneurs health insurance options.

7. **Maximize retirement savings.** Consider maximizing your contributions to retirement savings accounts while you are still employed. Take advantage of any employer matching programs or tax advantages provided by retirement plans. Building a solid retirement savings base will provide you with long-term financial security.

8. **Seek financial advice.** Talk to a financial planner who can assist with the shift from employee to entrepreneur. They can help you manage your finances and make smart choices during the transition.

Financial security allows you to take risks and invest in business growth without sacrificing your financial well-being. This will let you concentrate on developing your entrepreneurship skills and making your idea successful. It is also important to review and adjust your financial plan as circumstances change.

# Chapter 9: Networking with Like-minded People

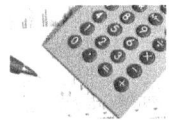

Networking with like-minded individuals is an invaluable strategy that extends beyond exchanging business cards. By actively engaging with others in my industry and entrepreneurial communities, I've found a wealth of knowledge and insights that I wouldn't have gained otherwise. By attending events and online communities, I learned from others' successes and failures.

I also discovered valuable lessons that helped refine my own entrepreneurial approach. These connections also serve as a support system during challenging times. They offer encouragement and valuable advice when navigating obstacles.

Building connections within the entrepreneurial community has led to exciting collaborations and partnerships. I worked with other entrepreneurs and found chances to collaborate on projects. Being a reliable and supportive community member can attract potential mentors and advisors to help grow my business.

Networking can also provide a platform to showcase your expertise and leadership in your industry. You can become a credible authority by speaking or writing. Here's an effective way to network with individuals who have similar interests:

1.  **Attend industry events and conferences.** Attend conferences, seminars, trade shows, and networking events that apply to your industry or entrepreneurial interests. These events provide opportunities to meet like-minded individuals, learn from industry experts, and stay updated on the latest trends and insights.

2.  **Join professional organizations or associations.** Join industry-specific professional organizations or associations where you can connect with fellow entrepreneurs, share experiences, and access resources and support. Take part in their events, workshops, or forums to engage with like-minded individuals and expand your network.

3.  **Utilize online networking platforms.** Leverage online platforms such as LinkedIn, industry-specific forums, and social media groups to connect with like-minded individuals. Engage in discussion,

share insights, and offer support to establish relationships with others in your field. Consider joining virtual networking events or webinars to connect with professionals beyond your local area.

4. **Seek out mentorship opportunities.** Look for mentors who have experience in your industry or have successfully pursued entrepreneurship. Mentors can offer guidance, share their insights, and provide valuable advice based on their own experiences. Reach out to potential mentors through networking events, professional organizations, or online platforms.

5. **Engage in collaborative projects or partnerships.** Look for opportunities to collaborate with like-minded individuals, projects, joint ventures, or partnerships. Collaborative efforts expand your network and provide avenues for sharing resources, knowledge, and expertise. Seek complementary skill sets or businesses that can enhance your own offerings.

6. **Offer support and value.** Networking is a two-way street. Be proactive in offering support, advice, and help to others in your network. Share your expertise, connect

people with relevant resources or contacts, and be genuinely interested in helping others succeed. By providing value to others, you strengthen your relationship and establish a positive reputation within your network.

7. **Foster meaningful connections.**
   Networking is not only about collecting business cards or adding social media contacts. Focus on building genuine relationships based on trust, mutual respect, and shared interests. Take time to connect on a deeper level, listen actively, and offer your support when needed. These meaningful connections can lead to long-term collaborations, referrals, or partnerships.

8. **Follow up and maintain relationships.**
   After meeting new contacts, follow up with them to express your appreciation for the connection and explore opportunities to stay in touch. Maintain your relationship regularly by reaching out, sharing relevant information or resources, and staying engaged in their professional journey. Consistent communication helps nurture relationships and keeps you at the top of their minds.

Networking is not necessarily about immediate gain, but it is about building a supportive and collaborative network of like-minded individuals. These people can offer guidance, inspiration, and opportunities for growth. Approach networking with a genuine interest in others and a willingness to contribute to the community. You'll find that it can be a powerful tool for personal and professional development as an entrepreneur. It creates new opportunities, encourages personal and professional development, and fosters collaboration among entrepreneurs.

# Chapter 10: Take the Plunge. Go for it!

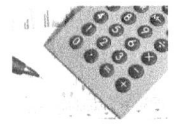

Embracing the entrepreneurial journey and starting your own business can be life-changing. Taking the plunge requires a combination of courage, determination, and passion for your vision. While life may fill the road ahead with uncertainties, those challenges provide opportunities for personal and professional growth. The process of building a business from the ground up may be stressful and demanding, but the satisfaction of turning your idea into reality and witnessing your vision come to life makes it all worthwhile.

As an entrepreneur, you will face unpredictable obstacles. Through overcoming these hurdles you will discover your true potential and resilience. The experience gained from each step, milestone, and lesson is worth more than just money. As Jeff Bezos said, "Pursue your passions. The risks are not as great as they seem to be." Remember, no risk, no reward. Here are a few reasons you should seize the opportunity and go for it:

1. **Confidence in your idea.** Believe in your business idea and have confidence in its potential for success. Conduct thorough research, validate your concept with your target customers, and gather feedback to strengthen your conviction. Trust in your ability and the value your business can offer.

2. **Preparedness and planning.** While being bold and taking action is essential, it's equally important to be prepared. Develop a solid business plan, create a strategic roadmap, and outline the steps to launch your business. Assess the risks and challenges you may face and have a contingency plan in place.

3. **Financial readiness.** As discussed earlier, Ensure you have established a financial strategy and saving plan. Having a financial safety net provides a buffer during the early stages of your business when revenue is probably limited. Be realistic about the financial commitment required and have a plan to sustain yourself during the initial growth phase.

4. **Support system.** Surround yourself with a supportive network of family, friends, mentors, or fellow entrepreneurs. Seek their

guidance, advice, and emotional support. Their encouragement and insights can help you navigate challenges and maintain motivation.

5.  **Embrace calculated risks.** Recognize that entrepreneurship involves taking calculated risks. Assess your business venture's risks and potential rewards and make informative decisions. Embrace a mindset that sees risks as opportunities for growth and learning. Understand that some level of risk is necessary for entrepreneurial success.

6.  **Learn from failure.** Understand that setbacks and failures are part of the entrepreneurial journey. Embrace a mindset that views failures as learning experiences and stepping stones to success. Analyze what went wrong, make necessary adjustments, and move forward. Adaptability and resilience are key attributes for entrepreneurs.

7.  **Start small and iterate.** Consider testing your product or starting with a smaller version of your business before committing fully. This approach allows you to gather feedback, validate your assumptions, and improve on real-world experiences.

Iteration and adaptation are common in entrepreneurship.

8. **Embrace continuous learning.** Commit to lifelong learning and professional development. Stay updated on industry trends, technology advancements, and evolving market needs. Improve your skills by taking courses, workshops, or online resources. Learning and adapting are essential for entrepreneurial success.

Taking the plunge requires courage, determination, and a belief in your entrepreneurial vision. Trust in your abilities, prepare yourself, seek support, embrace calculated risks, and maintain a continuous learning and growth mindset. Celebrate the excitement and possibilities of pursuing your dreams, and be open to the incredible opportunities that await you on your entrepreneurial journey. Take the plunge, embrace the challenges, and embark on this exciting journey. The rewards and possibilities that lie ahead are boundless.

# About the Author

Lynette Marshall-Harper is known as The Real Money Strategist™. She is a seasoned professional with 25 years of financial leadership. As a CFO, Financial Life Coach, REALTOR®, author, and speaker, she drives decisions through keen trend analysis, resource optimization, and sustainable solutions. A trusted advisor and mentor, she excels in team collaboration and executive guidance.